NATIONAL GEOGRAPHIC

T0042358

Who Lives Here?

Sue Whiting

Who lives here?

A polar bear lives here.

Who lives here?

A crab lives here.

Who lives here?

A fox lives here.

Who lives here?

A duck lives here.

Who lives here?

A giraffe lives here.

Who lives here?

A whale lives here.